I0617030

BUILT DIFFERENT

By **Jahkil Naeem Jackson**
Edited by **Kimberli J. Wilson, Chief Editor, Let's Book Up!**
Letsbookup.com
Designed by **Angel D'Amico-Baue**r
Cover Photo by **Charan Ingram**

DEDICATION

To Aunt Mary who has shown nothing but love and support for everything that I do. I can honestly say I see how proud you are of me and your energy makes me want to do good in everything I do. Thank you so much for all of your support! ❤️

To GG who has helped me grow with Project I Am. Without your support, I would not be where I am and I thank you for having my back even when I don't know it. 💪

To my guardian angels, my grandparents in heaven (Debra, Rick and Rodney) - thank you for passing down your strength and hustle to me! I hope that I'm making you proud. 🙏

To my parents, I AM because of you. 🙏

To Ms. Ariel Biggs, Thank You. 😍

INTRODUCTION
THIS SPACE IS FOR YOU

This book was created with one goal in mind: **to be a safe space for you.** A space where you don't have to have it all figured out.

A space where you're allowed to dream big, fight hard, fall sometimes, and still believe in everything you're becoming.

A space that reminds you that greatness isn't about being perfect, it's about being real, staying focused, and never giving up on yourself.

Here's what you need to know before you turn the page:
- **Your mental health matters.**
  - Taking care of your mind, your emotions, and your peace isn't extra, it's essential.
  - Before you chase success, chase balance. Before you grind harder, breathe deeper.
  - Self-care isn't selfish. It's survival.

- **You have what it takes.**
  - Even when the pressure gets heavy. Even when it feels like you're behind.
  - Believing in yourself, especially when it's hard is one of the greatest moves you'll ever make.

- **Adversity is part of the process.**
  - Setbacks don't mean you're not built for this. They mean you're *being built for something bigger.*
  - Every pivot, every struggle, every tough moment is shaping you, not breaking you.

This isn't a perfect path. It's your path.
Own it. Walk it. Fight for it.

And remember: you don't have to wait to be great, you already have greatness inside you.

Let's get started.

TABLE
OF CONTENTS

NO PLAN
NO PROGRESS

Before you can chase greatness, you have to define what greatness looks like for you. Greatness isn't just about winning trophies or going viral. It's about becoming the best version of yourself, consistently. Think about someone like Magic Johnson or Jaylen Brown. They're not just known for what they did on the court, they're respected for how they carry themselves off it. They are leaders, businessmen, and community builders. That's greatness.

But here's the thing: greatness doesn't happen by accident. It takes planning, discipline, and daily action. You can't just want it, you've got to work for it.

UNDERSTAND AND PRACTICE DISCIPLINE
Discipline is doing what needs to be done, even when you don't feel like doing it. It's easy to stay motivated when things are fun or when you're seeing quick results. But real discipline kicks in when it gets hard. I know this isn't easy. There are days when I'm tired from practice, mentally drained from school, or just not feeling it. But that's when I remind myself why I started. Without discipline, goals remain dreams. With it, dreams start becoming real.

SET GOALS AND CREATE A PLAN
A goal without a plan is just a wish. Set goals that challenge you without overwhelming you. Break them down into steps. Want to make the varsity team? What's your training schedule? Want to start a business? Who do you need to talk to? What's your first product or idea? When I was eight years old, I created my first vision board. I didn't have all the answers, but I knew I had to write it down and see it every day. That visual reminder helped me stay focused. And it works! Try it!

"Dreams don't work unless you do."

– Misty Copeland

DEVELOP HABITS AND ROUTINES

Goals are cool, but your grind is what gets you there. Big dreams don't carry you, your daily moves do. That's why routines matter. What does your morning look like? Are you making time to prep for school, workouts, or your hustle? Are you ending your day with intention, or just scrolling until you fall asleep? The smallest habits like making your bed, journaling and eating well, help shape a mindset of excellence.

STAY MOTIVATED

Motivation fades. That's just real. So you need ways to spark it again. Listen to something that fires you up. Surround yourself with people who remind you of your "why." Read stories about people who've done what you dream of doing. Often, I ask myself, "Why did I start?" That question helps me refocus. When you hit a wall and trust me, you will; it's that reason that will push you through.

Whether you're an athlete trying to level up, a student working to improve, or someone figuring it out one step at a time, remember this: planning your work and working your plan gives your dreams structure. Discipline gives them power.

Your future isn't just something that "happens" it's something you build. One goal. One plan. One action at a time.

"Success isn't always about greatness. It's about consistency. Consistent hard work leads to success. Greatness will come."

— Dwayne "The Rock" Johnson

LESSON LOCK-IN

Dreams without direction fades fast. When you create a plan, stay disciplined, and show up daily, even when it's hard; you turn dreams into progress. Greatness isn't one big moment; it's built through small, consistent actions.

Jahkil's Take

For me, goal setting started early. When I was eight, I made my first vision board and taped it to my wall. I didn't have it all figured out, but I knew I wanted to make a difference. Seeing those images every day reminded me to stay locked in, even when I didn't feel motivated. It wasn't about being perfect, it was about showing up, sticking to my plan, and doing something small every day to move forward. That's what helped me turn ideas into action.

TRY THIS:
VISION + ACTION
STARTER PACK

"A goal without a plan is just a wish."

First, take a minute to dream a little bigger. Think about something you want to accomplish — something that fires you up and maybe even makes you a little nervous (that's how you know it matters).

What's one big goal you have right now?
(Think: school, sports, business, creative dream, leadership, personal growth.)

My Big Goal:

_____

_____

_____

Now break it down into 3 small, doable steps you can take this week to move closer to it.
Even if the steps feel tiny, they count. Progress is progress.

Small Steps I Can Take This Week:

1. _____

2. _____

3. _____

Next, answer this:
Why does this goal matter to you?
(Write a sentence or two about why this goal is important and what reaching it would mean for you.)

My Why:

_____

_____

_____

Finally, make it real:
When will you take your first step? (Day + Time)
Ex: Monday after school, Wednesday during lunch, Saturday morning.

My Start Time:

_____

_____

_____

Quick Reminder:

Big dreams aren't built in one move.
They're built with _small steps, taken consistently,_
fueled by a real why.
Start small — just start. The future you want begins
with the first move you make today.

HEALTH
IS WEALTH

Photo by @dfilmz

13

Success isn't just about grinding and staying busy, it's also about taking care of you. Your body, your mind, and your emotions all play a role in how far you go. If one of those areas is off - it throws everything else off balance. So let's break it down:

MENTAL HEALTH: PROTECTING YOUR PEACE

A strong mindset can get you through the toughest seasons. But protecting your peace takes work. That means checking in with yourself, knowing when to unplug, and being honest when you're not okay. Normalize taking breaks when your mind is overwhelmed. You don't have to carry everything alone, talk to someone, journal your thoughts, or even take a walk to clear your head. Strength isn't just pushing through. Strength is knowing when to slow down, breathe, and regroup.

There are moments when everything feels loud; school, business, sport and life. I've learned that sometimes, protecting your peace means saying no to distractions or stepping away from the noise, even if it's just for a few minutes. It's not weakness, it's how I keep showing up strong.

EMOTIONAL HEALTH: FEEL WHAT YOU FEEL

Bottling things up might seem easier, but it usually leads to blow-ups or burnout. Emotional health means recognizing your feelings and learning how to respond vs. react. That could look like expressing your frustration through writing, venting to a trusted friend, or learning how to reframe negative thoughts. Everyone has off days. The key is not letting those days turn into your default setting. Protect your energy.

"You have to take care of yourself — your mental health, your physical health. It's all connected. And it all matters."
– Simone Biles

PHYSICAL HEALTH: FUEL THE HUSTLE

The way you treat your body affects how well you perform in school, sports, business, or anything else. Develop good exercise habits not just to look good, but to feel good. Regular movement fights depression, boosts confidence, and keeps your energy up. That doesn't mean you have to be in the gym 24/7. Find something you enjoy; basketball, dance, running, yoga, even walking. Pair it with rest, hydration, and solid nutrition.

BENEFITS OF CHOOSING A HEALTHY LIFESTYLE

- Improves focus and memory
- Boosts energy and motivation
- Fights stress and anxiety
- Helps you bounce back from challenges
- Builds discipline and consistency
- Supports long-term success

Choosing a healthy lifestyle doesn't mean being perfect. It means being intentional. It means caring enough about your future to care for yourself now. Your health is your power. Protect it, build on it, and let it fuel your greatness.

"You don't have to see the whole staircase, just take the first step. Be brave enough to take that step."
– Martin Luther King, Jr

LESSON LOCK-IN

You can't pour from an empty cup. Prioritizing your mental, emotional, and physical health isn't selfish, it's necessary. When you take care of yourself, you show up stronger in every part of your life.

Jahkil's Take

There were times when I was doing so much; from school, basketball, business, and events, that I didn't even notice how drained I was. I thought grinding nonstop meant I was doing the right thing, but I realized I wasn't taking care of my mental or physical health. Now, I am intentional about checking in with myself. I meditate, I take breaks, and I give myself space to rest. Being healthy isn't just physical, it's about keeping your mind and emotions balanced too. That's my strategy for staying in the game for the long run.

TRY THIS:
ENERGY CHECK

*"You can't pour into your dreams
if you're running on empty."*

Before you chase goals, crush games, or stack wins — you've got to check in with *you*. Your mind, your emotions, and your body are your foundation. If you're drained, everything else feels heavier. If you're fueled up, everything feels possible.

First, Rate Your Current Energy Levels:

- **Mental Health:** 😃 🙂 😐 😟 😩

(Focused, clear, overwhelmed, stressed, exhausted)

- **Emotional Health:** 😃 🙂 😐 😟 😩

(Positive, steady, uncertain, frustrated, down)

- **Physical Health:** 😃 🙂 😐 😟 😩

(Energized, okay, tired, sluggish, drained)

Next, Reflect on This:

What's one area you're feeling strongest in?

_____

What's one area you want to strengthen this week?

_____

Now, Build Your Energy Plan:

Answer these questions to create a quick self-care action plan for the week:

1. What's one small thing you can do to recharge mentally?
(Example: take a 10-minute phone break, journal, set a daily goal)

2. What's one small thing you can do to recharge emotionally?
(Example: vent to a trusted friend, write out your wins, set boundaries)

3. What's one small thing you can do to recharge physically?
(Example: stretch before bed, drink more water, move your body)

Quick Reminder:

You don't have to overhaul your life overnight.
One small move toward better health can flip your whole energy for the better.

Protect your peace. Power your purpose. Then go chase your dreams.

FIND YOUR FLOW
DISCOVERING WHAT DRIVES YOU

A lot of people will tell you what you should do. But real success - It starts when you figure out what you want to do. What lights you up? What comes naturally? What makes you feel like your best self? That's called finding your flow — when you're doing something that doesn't just feel good, but also feels right.

The journey starts with exploring what you're good at, what excites you, and what makes you different. You don't need to have all the answers today — but you do need to start paying attention.

TRY DIFFERENT THINGS — ON PURPOSE

The only way to know what you're good at is to try stuff. That means stepping outside your comfort zone, signing up for things that feel new, and asking questions along the way. You might find out you're into art, coding, public speaking, mentoring, photography, or even entrepreneurship. And if you try something and don't like it – cool, that's one thing crossed off the list. Keep moving.

The more you explore, the more doors you'll open — some that might lead to your future.

PAY ATTENTION TO WHAT COMES NATURALLY

Sometimes we overlook our strengths because they come easy. But that's exactly what you should lean into. Are you the person who always organizes group projects? Do your friends come to you for advice? Can you speak, write, draw, or build without overthinking it?

These natural gifts aren't random, they're clues. Your talents are trying to tell you something. Listen.

Photo by @shotbyralph

"Don't be afraid of new arenas. You were born to stand out."

— LeBron James

ASK YOURSELF THE RIGHT QUESTIONS

If you don't know where to start, these questions will help you get clear:

- What am I naturally good at — without even trying?
- What do I enjoy so much, I lose track of time when I do it?
- What problems do I care about solving?
- If money wasn't an issue, what would I spend my time doing?

Your answers don't have to be perfect. Just be honest. Self-discovery is a process, not a pop quiz.

IT'S OKAY IF THE PATH LOOKS DIFFERENT

Don't stress if your passion doesn't look like everyone else's. Not everyone's path is school-to-career, or sports-to-scholarship. Some people build businesses. Some start movements. Some create. Some lead quietly. Your path can be as unique as you are and that's what makes it powerful.

Comparison is the quickest way to lose your confidence. Don't chase someone else's highlight reel, build your own legacy.

SHARPEN YOUR STRENGTHS

Once you know what lights you up, go all in. Study it. Practice it. Ask for mentorship. Look for ways to grow. Talent might come naturally, but excellence takes work. Even the best athletes, artists, speakers, and creators started with curiosity — and then kept showing up.

You don't have to be great right away. But if you keep sharpening what you've got, you'll surprise yourself with how far you can go.

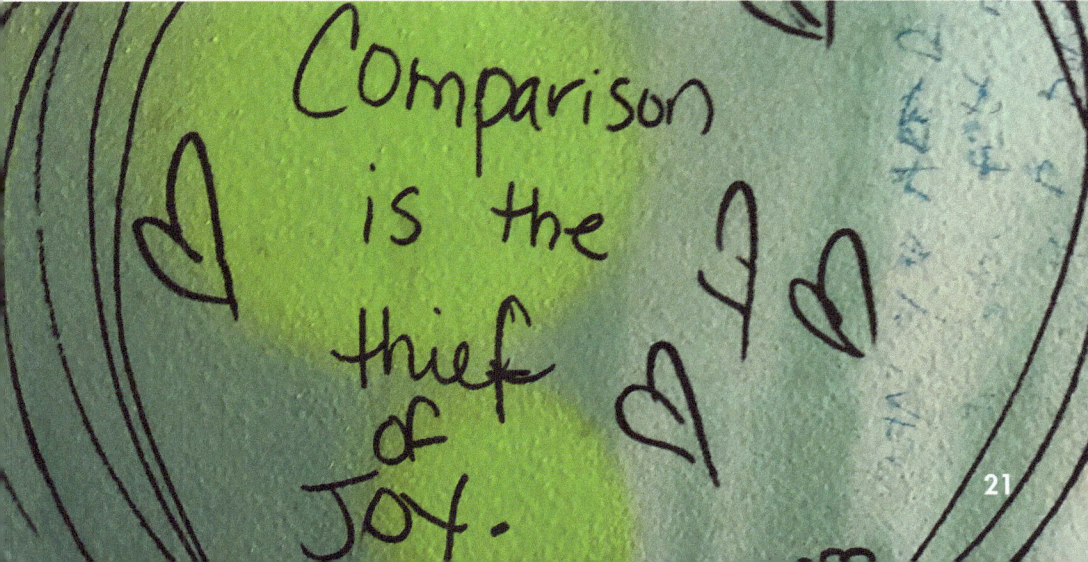

LESSON LOCK-IN

Finding your flow starts with curiosity. Try new things, trust your talents, and stay honest about what brings you joy. Your passion is a clue. Your potential is real. And your path? That's yours to discover — and build.

Jahkil's Take

I was exposed to a lot growing up: tap dance, break dance, soccer, acting, modeling, coding, and of course, basketball. Anytime I showed even a little bit of interest, my family found a program or opportunity for me to try it out. That kind of exposure made a huge difference. It helped me figure out what I liked, what I didn't, and what I wanted to do more of.

Trying new things gave me confidence. Traveling and meeting other young people who had similar goals or mindsets inspired me to keep growing. I didn't always know what my "thing" was, but I stayed open. And over time, I found what felt right — and I leaned all the way in.

>>>>> TRY THIS: <<<<<
CURIOSITY CHECK-IN

"You won't know what you're good at until you give yourself permission to try."

Before you move on, hit pause. Sometimes the biggest moves start with a little curiosity — that moment where you wonder, *"Could I be good at that?"* or *"What if I tried?"*

The truth is: you don't discover your gifts by waiting.
You discover them by doing.

Step 1: What Sparks Your Curiosity?

What are 3 things you're curious about but haven't tried yet?
(They could be hobbies, skills, careers, passions, or causes you care about. Big or small — all curiosity counts.)

My Curiosity List:

1. _____

2. _____

3. _____

Step 2: Dig Deeper

Pick one thing from your list that stands out the most — the one that makes you lean in a little closer.

Which one did you pick?

1. _____

Now answer these quick questions to explore it even more:

- Why does this interest you?

- What's one thing you already know about it?

- What's one question you still have about it?

23

Step 3: Move from Curiosity to Action

Here's your challenge:
(Find one small way to explore that curiosity this week.
Ideas:

- Watch a YouTube video about it
- Talk to someone who's already doing it
- Try it for one hour
- Read an article or find a beginner's guide
- Sign up for a free class or event

What's your action step?

_____

When will you do it? (Day + Time)

_____

Quick Reminder:

**You don't have to be great to start.
You have to start to find your greatness.**

Stay curious. Stay open. The next move you
try might just change your future.

PREPARATION
= POWER

Photo by @goard_official

If there's one thing that can throw a dream off track, it's not being prepared when your moment comes. Opportunities don't always give you a heads-up, they show up when they show up. That's why it's important to stay ready, even when it feels like no one's watching. Because when your name is called, it's already too late to prepare.

AVOIDING BAD HABITS

Let's be real. Bad habits can sneak in quickly: procrastination, negative thinking, comparing yourself to others, skipping workouts, or getting caught up in the wrong crowd. A way to stay strong is by protecting your mindset and your space. That means surrounding yourself with people who push you to be better, not pull you down. It also means knowing when to say no. Not every opportunity is good for you, and every person does not deserve your time.

CREATE YOUR CHEAT CODES

We all need cheat codes, not for skipping steps, but for staying locked in. These can be reminders, routines, or habits that keep you focused. Maybe it's writing your goals on your mirror, so you see them every morning. Maybe it's turning your phone on Do Not Disturb during homework or workouts. Maybe it's setting a playlist that gets you in the zone. Little hacks can make a big difference when your motivation dips.

MANAGING PRE-GAME NERVES

Whether you're stepping onto a basketball court, presenting in class, or applying for something important, nerves are real. A way to manage pre-performance anxiety is through preparation. Visualize your success before it happens. Take deep breaths. Remind yourself of how much you've already overcome. Nerves are normal, they just mean you care. But they don't have to control you.

EMBRACING A GROWTH MINDSET

A growth mindset means believing that your skills and talents can improve with effort. Instead of saying, "I'm not good at this," say, "I'm still learning." Mistakes don't mean failure, they're proof that you're trying. Whether you're an athlete, a student, or still figuring it all out, embracing growth allows you to keep evolving without pressure to be perfect.

STAYING RESILIENT WHILE WAITING YOUR TURN
One major lesson I've learned is how to wait my turn. And not just wait, but work while waiting. That's the difference between being ready and being rusty. You might not always get picked first. You might not get that starting spot, that scholarship or that big break right away. But that doesn't mean it's not coming. While you're waiting, someone else is watching. Coaches, mentors, future bosses, they notice effort; even when you think no one sees it.

PREPARING FOR COMPETITION
Whether you're competing in sports, preparing for an exam, or going after a leadership position, preparation matters. Study the game, the material, or the task ahead of you. Ask questions. Practice. Know your strengths and sharpen your weaknesses. When competition shows up, you don't want to guess — you want to respond with confidence.

OVERCOMING ADVERSITY
Adversity isn't optional, it's guaranteed. What matters is how you respond. When things fall apart, do you fold or fight? One of the strongest things you can do is bounce back. Resilience means refusing to let setbacks define you. Instead of asking "Why me?" Ask, "What lesson am I to receive?" Challenges build character. They test your grit. And more often than not, they prepare you for something greater.

BUILDING A POSITIVE ROUTINE
Success isn't just about big wins, it's about small habits done consistently. Start with your daily routine. Are you sleeping enough? Drinking water? Stretching after workouts? Taking time to breathe and recalibrate? These might seem like small things, but they build your foundation. A strong routine keeps your body and mind ready for the pressure that comes with chasing big dreams.

Being excellent in school, sports, business, or leadership isn't about luck, it's about preparation, persistence, and having a mindset that won't quit. Whether your dream is to play in college, start a company, or change the world, remember - stay ready, so you don't have to get ready.

"If you stay ready, you ain't gotta get ready."

– Lena Waithe

LESSON LOCK-IN

Opportunities don't wait for you to be "ready." Preparation, consistency, and mindset are your advantage. Stay focused, protect your habits, and trust that the work you do in the dark will shine when it's your time.

Jahkil's Take

There's been moments where an opportunity came out of nowhere, a big speaking event, a campaign shoot, even a meeting with someone important. If I hadn't been preparing behind the scenes, I wouldn't have been ready. One thing I've learned is that you can't wait for the moment to get serious. You've got to stay serious so when your name is called, you're not scrambling. I stay ready by keeping my routines tight and my mindset strong — that way, I don't miss my shot when it comes.

Because here's the truth: you miss 100% of the shots you don't take. So stay ready, keep shooting, and believe the right moment is on its way.

>>>>> TRY THIS: <<<<<
READINESS CHECK

*"Champions are made
in the unseen hours."*

Everyone sees the moment you shine — but not everyone sees the late nights, the early mornings, and the quiet work that made it possible.

The truth?
How you prepare when no one's watching is what shapes how you perform when everyone's watching.

Step 1: What's Coming Up?

Think about something important you've got coming soon — a test, a tryout, a performance, an interview, a big event, or even a goal you're working toward.

What is it?

Step 2: Rate Your Readiness

Be real with yourself:
On a scale of 1 to 10, how ready do you feel right now?

(1 = not ready at all | 10 = bring it on)

My score:

Step 3: Build Your Game Plan

Nobody goes from a 5 to a 10 overnight. But you can always level up a little — and a little makes a big difference.

What's one thing you could do to move 1 or 2 points higher on that scale?
(Think: more practice, a study session, a checklist, extra sleep, visualization, reaching out for help.)

What's one small step you can take TODAY to start preparing stronger?

Step 4: Visualize It

Take 30 seconds.
Close your eyes and imagine yourself locked in and ready — calm, confident, and performing at your best.

Picture the success before it happens.

That's part of training your mind for the win.

Quick Reminder:

You don't rise to the moment — you rise to the level of your preparation.

Lay the foundation now, so when your name gets called, you're already built for it.

THE POWER
OF THE PIVOT

As you navigate through the world, you will encounter numerous situations that require you to adapt and adjust. Just like in sports, where the pivot foot allows players to change direction while maintaining their balance; the ability to adjust is crucial for success both on and off the court.

LEAN INTO CHANGE

Change is the one thing in life that's guaranteed. It might be uncomfortable, unpredictable, or even scary, but it's also where growth happens. Whether it's transferring schools, switching teams, or adjusting to a new role, your ability to lean into change will define your strength. If you fight change, you stay stuck. If you lean into it, you grow.

I had to make the decision to transfer schools halfway through high school, not because I wanted to, but because I realized I wasn't in the best environment to grow. It wasn't easy leaving what I knew, but I had to choose my future over my comfort zone. That decision helped me level up, on the court and in the classroom.

BUILD RESILIENCE

Resilience isn't about never falling, it's about getting back up every single time you do. Life will throw challenges your way, and you won't always be able to control what happens. But what you can control is how you respond. You can use setbacks as setups. You can bounce back stronger. And you can remind yourself: this moment doesn't define you, your response does.

"It's okay to outgrow people, places, and paths. Pivoting is part of the process."

– Elaine Welteroth

ADAPTING TO NEW ENVIRONMENTS

Starting over or walking into a new room can be nerve-wracking. New classrooms, new coaches, new teammates all come with pressure. But don't let fear keep you small. Introduce yourself. Ask questions. Pay attention. Be open to learning the ropes without feeling like you have to prove everything right away. Confidence grows when you give yourself permission to be new, and still show up.

When I transferred to a new school, everything was different, the classes, the people, and the vibe. I had to adjust fast. I stayed focused on why I made the move and kept my head up, even when it felt uncomfortable. Change pushed me to grow.

BALANCE IS A REAL SKILL

Balancing academics, sports, business, and your social life takes practice. And truthfully, you won't always get it right. But that doesn't mean it's impossible. It just means you need systems. Use a planner. Set boundaries. Learn when to say yes and when to say no. Prioritize what matters most. Staying organized and focused helps you manage your responsibilities and protect your peace.

EMBRACE GROWTH AND DEVELOPMENT

Every season of life offers new lessons. Stay curious. Be coachable. Ask yourself: What can I learn from this moment? How can I grow here? Whether you're winning or struggling, there's always something to gain. Growth mindset means you don't have to be perfect, just willing to learn and improve. And improvement, over time, leads to success.

LESSON LOCK-IN

Pivoting doesn't mean quitting, it means adjusting your angle so you can keep moving forward, even when things don't go as planned. Stay grounded in your purpose, be flexible in your approach, and remember: growth lives outside your comfort zone.

Jahkil's Take

Making the decision to transfer schools was one of the biggest pivots I've had to make. It meant leaving behind comfort, friendships, and a routine I was used to. But I realized that staying in the same place wasn't helping me grow the way I needed to. It taught me that sometimes, the best move is the hardest one. Change might feel risky but staying stuck is risky too. So when it's time to pivot, academically, athletically, or in life; just trust your instincts, stay grounded, and it's okay to change direction as long as your purpose stays solid.

>>>>>> TRY THIS: <<<<<<
-PIVOT-POWER-REFLECTION

"You can pivot without losing your purpose."

Change isn't weakness.
Pivoting doesn't mean you're lost — it means you're strong enough to
adjust your path while keeping your mission alive.

Sometimes life forces you to make a move you didn't expect:
Switching schools.
Leaving a team.
Letting go of friendships.
Starting something new from scratch.
It's hard — but it's also where growth lives.

Step 1: Reflect on Your Pivot

Think of a time you had to adjust:
(Maybe it was recently. Maybe it was a big deal. Maybe it was
something quiet that still mattered.)

What happened?

Step 2: Find the Lesson

Every pivot teaches you something — even if you didn't realize it
right away.

Maybe you got tougher. Maybe you found your real people. Maybe you
learned you're stronger than you thought.

What did you learn from that experience?

35

Step 3: Pay It Forward

Imagine someone younger than you — or even your younger self — going through a big change right now.

What would you tell them to remind them that pivots are part of the process?

What advice would you give someone else facing a big change?

Quick Reminder:

Growth doesn't always feel good at first.

But every pivot — every adjustment — shapes you into someone wiser, tougher, and more prepared for what's next.

Trust the shift. Trust your purpose. Use the pivot to move forward.

THE FINAL SECONDS:
PRESSURE, PREPARATION, AND PERFORMANCE

In life, just like in sports, there are moments that test everything you've got, moments when the pressure is high, the clock is ticking, and all eyes are on you. These "last second shots" don't just happen on the court, they show up in the classroom, in interviews, during performances, or when you're chasing a dream that feels just out of reach. What matters most in those moments isn't just talent, it is preparation, confidence, and the mindset to rise under pressure. In this chapter, we'll break down how to stay ready for your moment, so when it comes, you're not only prepared, you're clutch.

EMBRACE THE CHALLENGE
Pressure doesn't have to break you it can build you. Every challenge you face is a chance to prove to yourself what you're made of. Instead of avoiding hard things, lean into them. Growth comes from stretching beyond your comfort zone. If you're never challenged, you're never changed.

When things feel tough, remind yourself that diamonds are made under pressure. The discomfort you feel now could be shaping you into someone stronger, sharper, and more focused. Don't run from the hard, face it head-on.

HANDLE PRESSURE LIKE A PRO
Pressure is part of greatness. The key is learning how to respond, not react. Whether it's the final seconds of a game or the final minutes of a test, staying calm under pressure comes down to three things: preparation, confidence, and breath.

- **Preparation** builds trust in your ability.
- **Confidence** grows when you remember your hard work.
- **Breathing** slows down panic and helps you focus.

Start practicing now, in small ways. Control your breathing when you're stressed. Ground yourself in moments of chaos. Train your body and mind to stay calm, so pressure becomes fuel, not fear.

BUILD MENTAL TOUGHNESS

Mental toughness isn't about pretending everything is easy, it's about pushing forward when it's not. It's saying, "I'm tired, but I'm not done." It's showing up, locked in, when the situation calls for your best. You build it by doing hard things on purpose, the extra reps, the late-night study sessions, and the early morning alarms. Mental strength is a muscle, and the more you use it, the stronger it gets.

You don't become mentally tough overnight. It comes from small wins and from doing what needs to be done; even when you don't feel like it. And over time, those small wins add up and turn into confidence under pressure.

VISUALIZE SUCCESS

What you see in your mind matters. Visualization is a powerful tool, athletes use it, performers use it, and you can too. Imagine yourself succeeding in the situation you're walking into. See the shot going in. See the "A" on your paper. See yourself staying calm and confident. The brain doesn't know the difference between a real experience and a vividly imagined one. Use that to your advantage.

Try this: take one minute before a big moment and close your eyes. Play it out in your mind like a highlight reel. Hear the sound, feel the nerves, then feel the win, that repetition creates mental reps that can boost real-life confidence.

Photo by @snapvisualsofficial

MASTER TIME MANAGEMENT

When you're chasing big goals, time matters. It's not about being busy, it's about being intentional with your time. Make a schedule. Prioritize what matters most. Set timers, reminders, or download apps that help you focus. Eliminate distractions when it's time to lock in. The people who perform at the highest level aren't just talented, they know how to manage their minutes.

Time is a tool, not an enemy. The more you learn how to control your time, the more control you'll feel over your day, your energy, and your results. Build habits that help you win, even on the busiest days.

ALWAYS GIVE 100%

Whether it's the first quarter or the final play, how you do one thing is how you do everything. Don't wait until it's "your moment" to give your all. Bring intensity, focus, and effort from start to finish. That's what separates good from great. Consistency builds momentum. And when that last second shot does come? You'll be ready because you've been giving your best the whole time.

Even when no one's watching, give your full effort. It's the grind behind the scene that creates the highlight moments everyone sees. Treat every play, every rep, every moment like it matters — because it does.

LESSON LOCK-IN

Your big moment won't come with a warning. That's why you give 100% from the start. Embrace pressure, sharpen your focus, manage your time, and visualize your win. When the game is on the line, in life or on the court, make sure you're the one they can count on.

Jahkil's Take

I've had moments where everything came down to the wire, a tight game, a live interview, even a huge decision. The thing that helped me the most wasn't just talent, it was all the work no one saw. The late nights, the early mornings, the stuff I did when no one was watching. Pressure doesn't scare me like it used to, because I've trained for it. I visualize the outcome I want, I breathe through the nerves, and I remind myself that I've put in the work. Whether I'm speaking on stage or dribbling down the court, I try to give 100% the whole way - not just at the buzzer. Because if you wait until the last second to give your best, you've already waited too long.

TRY THIS:
ALL-IN
SELF-CHECK

"Give 100% all game long —
not just when the buzzer's near."

Pick one area where you've been holding back or going halfway (school, sports, relationships, business, etc.)

Where have you been going half-speed?

_____

_____

What would "100% effort" look like in that area this week?

Bring that energy. No more saving your best for later.

Photo by @da.nnyt

You've made it this far and that's something to be proud of. The growth, the challenges, the mindset shifts… all of it brought you to this moment. But just like in sports, it's not enough to start strong but you've got to finish strong, too. The last stretch is where focus matters most. In this chapter, we're talking about the closeout: how to lock in, hold your ground, and seal the win when the pressure's on. Because success isn't just about how you begin, it's about how you finish.

STAY LOCKED IN

When you're close to the finish line, distractions hit harder. Your mind starts drifting, people start celebrating too early, and focus slips. That's when mistakes happen. The closeout is all about staying mentally locked in, not letting up just because you're ahead. Whether it's a school project, a business pitch, or the final moments of a game, the ability to stay present and sharp is what separates champions from everyone else.

Remind yourself: the job's not done yet. Celebrate later, execute now. You didn't come this far just to coast through the last stretch. This is where your focus gets sharper and your habits take over.

EXECUTE WITH PURPOSE

Late-game moments demand more than just effort, they require execution. This is where your systems, your practice, and your preparation come into play. What's the next step? What do you need to finish strong? In school, it might mean double-checking that final essay before you hit submit. In life, it could mean making that extra call, reviewing the game plan, or tightening up details that others ignore.

You've already done the work, now it's about finishing it with intention. The way you execute the ending leaves a lasting impression. Finish like you want to be remembered.

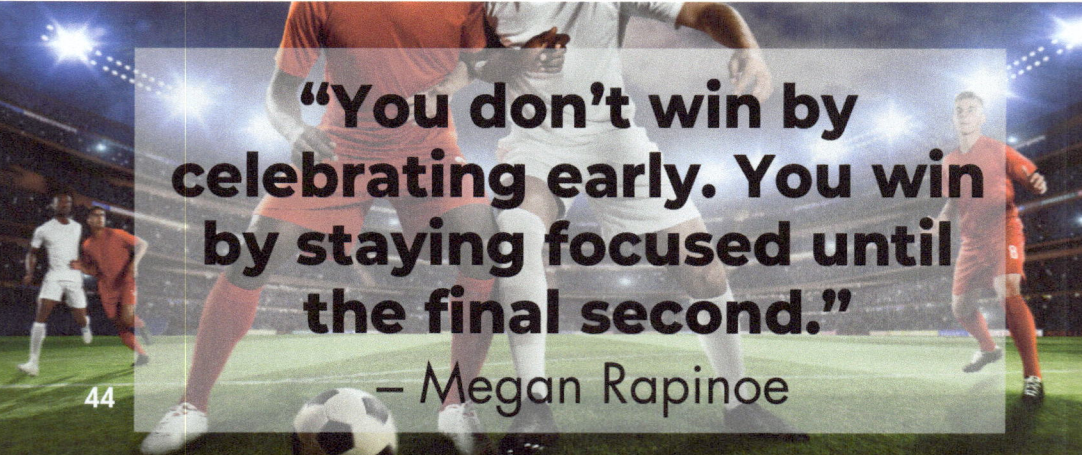

"You don't win by celebrating early. You win by staying focused until the final second."
— Megan Rapinoe

44

MANAGE THE CLOCK

Time is one of your biggest assets and can be your biggest enemy, depending on how you use it. Learn how to pace yourself, especially when pressure builds. Don't rush when patience is needed. Don't hesitate when it's time to strike. Managing your time in the final moments means knowing when to slow things down, when to turn it up, and when to finish with power.

Time doesn't pause when you're tired, so make every minute count. Protect your energy and don't waste time on distractions that won't matter tomorrow. Champions don't just count minutes, they make minutes count.

MENTAL FORTITUDE IN CRUNCH TIME

When it gets hard, your mindset has to get harder. Mental fortitude is the voice in your head that says, "Let's finish what we started." It's refusing to quit when you're tired, discouraged, or tempted to coast. Crunch time exposes your mental game and it's where resilience shows up.

The ability to stay calm under pressure isn't a gift, it's a skill. You build it every time you choose discipline over comfort. Don't fold. Lock in. This is where growth happens.

TRUST YOURSELF

In the final moments, you can't afford to doubt yourself. Trust the work you put in. Trust the preparation, the grind, the late nights, and the early mornings. You don't need to be perfect you just need to believe you're ready.

Second-guessing yourself takes energy away from execution. You've earned this moment, now step into it with confidence. You got here for a reason so act like it.

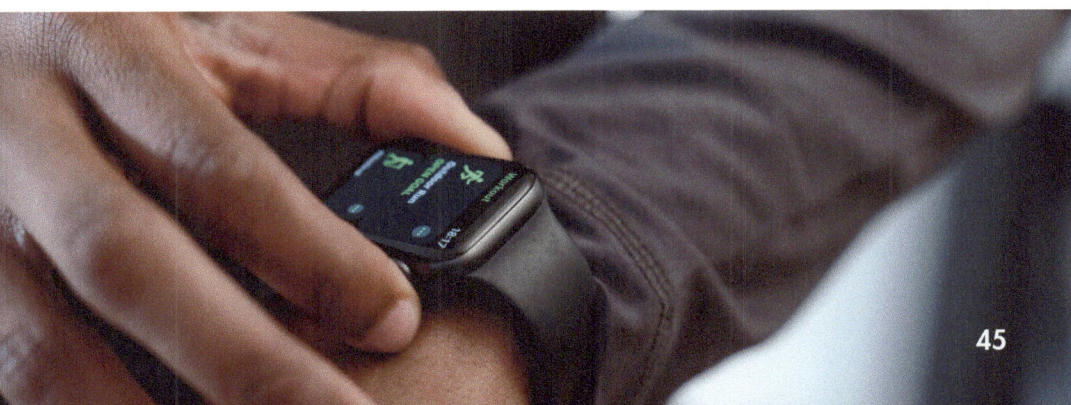

CELEBRATE, BUT DON'T GET COMFORTABLE

It's okay to feel proud of how far you've come but don't let celebration turn into complacency. Finishing strong means staying humble and hungry. You can acknowledge your wins and still keep your foot on the gas. Too many people lose momentum because they start dancing before the clock hits zero.

Celebrate the progress after the win is secured. Stay sharp until the very end. Success doesn't come from one great move it comes from seeing it all the way through.

CLUTCH CLOSEOUT CHECKLIST

Use this list anytime you're nearing the end of a goal, challenge, or project. Keep it close, this is your personal closeout game plan:

- ☐ Am I still focused, or have I started coasting?
- ☐ What's the one thing I need to finish strong today?
- ☐ Am I managing my time or letting time manage me?
- ☐ What does "100% effort" look like for this final push?
- ☐ Have I taken a moment to visualize the win?
- ☐ Am I trusting myself and my preparation?
- ☐ Have I earned my celebration or do I still have work to do?

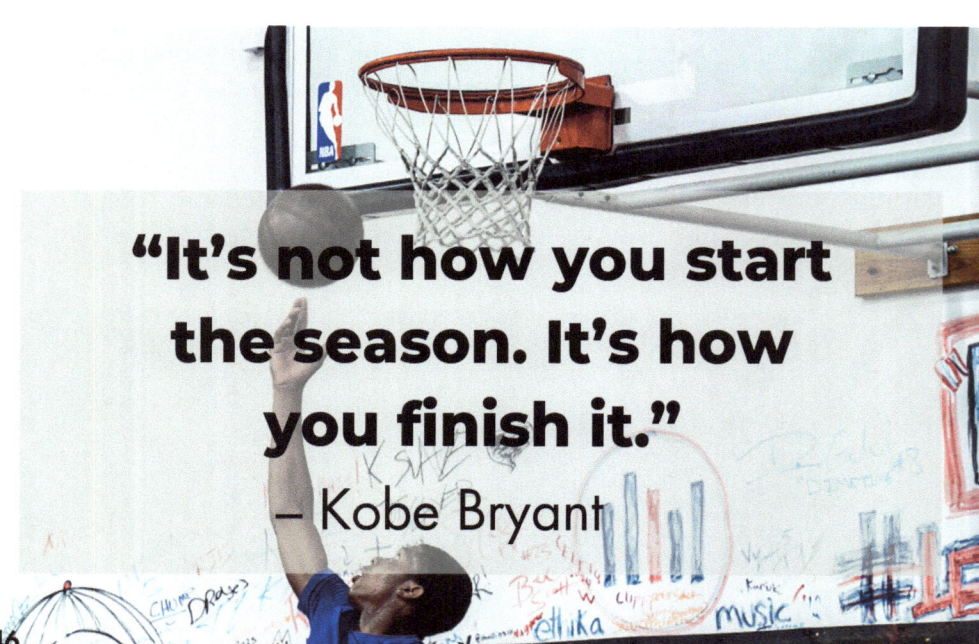

"It's not how you start the season. It's how you finish it."

– Kobe Bryant

LESSON LOCK-IN

Wins are earned at the finish. Lock in, trust your process, and don't let up until the final whistle blows. Success isn't just about how you start, it's about how you close. So finish strong, finish focused, and finish proud.

Jahkil's Take

One thing I've learned is that people remember how you finish. I've been in games where we were up big and let it slip because we relaxed too early. I've also had moments where staying locked in helped me deliver when it mattered most; whether it was finishing strong in school, wrapping up a big project, or closing out a speaking event. What's helped me most is reminding myself: the job isn't done until it's done. I trust my preparation, stay present, and push through to the last second. Because how you close the game often defines the whole story.

TRY THIS:
FINISH LINE FOCUS

"Success isn't about starting strong — it's about closing strong."

Starting is exciting.
But finishing — that's where champions are made.
Lots of people dream big and sprint out the gate... but the real ones stay locked in until the job is done.

Step 1: What Needs to Be Finished?

Think about something you started recently — a project, a goal, a commitment you made to yourself. Big or small, it matters.

Project/Goal:

Step 2: What's the Move?

Now ask yourself:

What's the ONE next step you can take this week to move closer to the finish line?

(Keep it real and keep it doable.)

_____

_____

_____

_____

_____

_____

_____

Quick Reminder:

It's easy to get hyped about the start.
It's powerful to stay hyped about the finish.
Small moves lead to big wins — stack
yours this week.

Close it out strong.

Success isn't built alone.
It's built on lessons — from the people who came before us, the ones who failed, fought, and figured it out.

These aren't just quotes.
They're keys given to us by legends — athletes, leaders, game-changers — who learned the hard way and chose to leave the door cracked open for the next generation — For you.

Take what you need. Hold on to what speaks to you.
Because after this, you'll hear from me — unfiltered, real, no game face.

Before you step into my final truth, here's the wisdom that helped shape the mindset it takes to keep going.

"You have to believe in your plan and stick to it. Never quit, never give up." — **Serena Williams**

"Don't wait to be great." — **Jahkil Jackson**

"You don't have to be perfect, but you do have to be honest about how you're doing. That's where real strength lives." — **Michelle Obama**

"You're always one decision away from a totally different life." — **Magic Johnson**

"I don't want other people to decide who I am. I want to decide that for myself." — **Emma Watson**

"Passion is energy. Feel the power that comes from focusing on what excites you." — **Oprah Winfrey**

"It's not about being the best. It's about being better than you were yesterday." — **Unknown**

"I stay ready so I don't have to get ready. You never know when the moment will come — and when it does, I'm going to own it." – **Chloe Kim**

"Sometimes you have to be your own hero. You've got to rescue yourself." — **Michael B. Jordan**

"You can't be hesitant about who you are." — **Viola Davis**

"When you stay ready, you don't have to get ready." — **Will Smith**

"The future belongs to those who prepare for it today." — **Malcolm X**

"I can accept failure, everyone fails at something. But I can't accept not trying." — **Michael Jordan**

"The moment you give up is the moment you let someone else win." — **Kobe Bryant**

"I really think a champion is defined not by their wins but by how they can recover when they fall." — **Serena Williams**

"Champions keep playing until they get it right." — **Billie Jean King**

"Believe in something. Even if it means sacrificing everything." — **Colin Kaepernick**

"Your story is what you have, what you will always have. It is something to own." — **Michelle Obama**

JAHKIL UNFILTERED:

THE TRUTH THEY DIDN'T TEACH IN CLASS.

Before we close out for real, I want to share some truths I've learned during high school; lessons that didn't come from a textbook, but from life. These are things that shaped me, challenged me, and showed me who I am - and who I'm becoming. If you're a teen trying to figure it out, I hope this helps. If you're an adult reading this, I hope it reminds you that we're watching. We're paying attention. And how you treat young people matters.

1. PRESSURE IS REAL.

Peer pressure, performance pressure, pressure to live up to expectations, and the pressure of just being a young Black man in Chicago — it's heavy. It's something I've had to face in a lot of different ways. What's helped me is surrounding myself with people who respect me, not just for what I do, but for who I am. When the pressure builds, your circle matters. Choose wisely.

2. SCHOOL IS WHAT YOU MAKE IT.

There were times when school felt impossible, overwhelming and isolating. But I realized I didn't have to go through it alone. There are people out there who want to help; like teachers, counselors, mentors, and tutors. You just have to find them, ask for support, and let them show up for you. It's not weak to ask for help, it's smart.

3. SUCCESS TAKES A VILLAGE.

No one makes it alone. That's something I've learned over and over again. Even if you feel like you're on your own right now, I promise there are people out there who are like-minded, who are grinding like you, and want to build with you. Look for people who believe in your mission and want to see you grow, not just benefit from your glow.

4. NOT EVERYONE HAS YOUR BEST INTERESTS.

This one's tough to write because sometimes the people who say they have your back are the same ones who end up hurting you the most. There were adults in my life who were supposed to protect me, guide me, and stand by me - but instead, they used me, misled me, and tried to control my path for their own benefit. And I see it now for what it is. That kind of betrayal hits different when it comes from people you were told you could trust.

To the adults who act like they care but only show up when it benefits them: young people are not your marketing tool, your project, or your stepping stone. We're human beings with futures, feelings, and purpose. You don't get to dim someone's light and still call it mentorship. Do better — because the damage you cause is real.

Even through that pain, I've learned how to rise. I've learned to protect my peace, trust my gut, and bounce back. You don't let betrayal define you. You let it refine you.

> **"I'm going to be who I am, and if people like it, that's great. And if they don't, it's okay."**
>
> – Kyrie Irving

www.ingramcontent.com/pod-product-compliance
Lightning Source LLC
Chambersburg PA
CBHW040858120626
46551CB00001B/70